First in Space

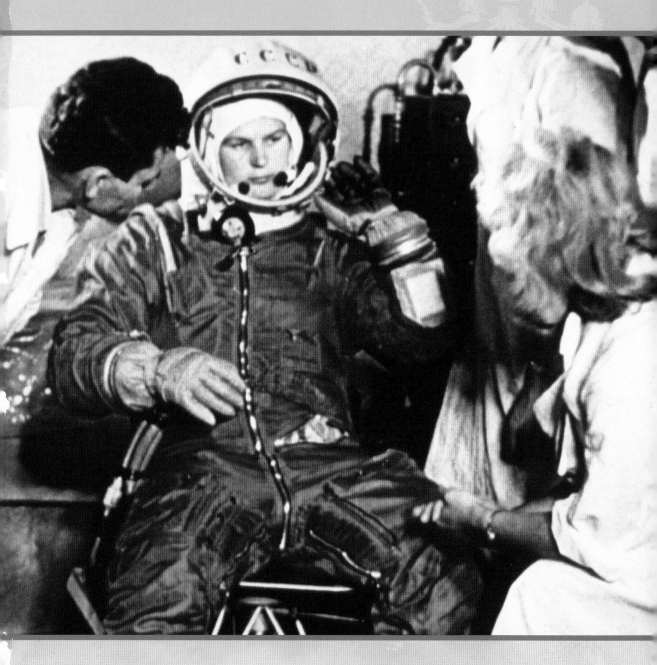

Written by Claire Owen

Russia

My name is Mikhail. I live in Moscow, Russia. Most people know that the United States was the first country to send astronauts to the Moon. Did you know, however, that Russia had many important "space firsts" in the 1950s and 1960s?

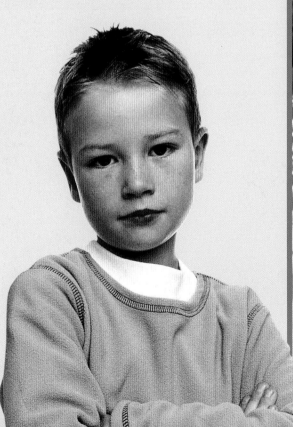

Contents

Wherever you see me, you'll find activities to try and questions to answer.

An Impossible Dream?

For centuries, people dreamed of traveling into space. Many stories were written about journeying through space and visiting other planets or moons. But until the late 1950s, these stories were simply science fiction. No one had ever managed to travel more than a few kilometers above Earth.

Outer space begins about 80 to 100 kilometers above Earth. There is no clearly defined boundary, because Earth's atmosphere gets thinner very gradually.

science fiction made-up stories about space travel, creatures from outer space, or future worlds

The first hot-air balloon that carried passengers rose 25 meters into the air and stayed there for about 4 minutes. This took place in France in 1783.

Did You Know?

The record height reached by a hot-air balloon was set in 1961. Two U.S. Navy officers rode a balloon to a height of 34.7 kilometers and parachuted back to Earth.

Konstantin Tsiolkovsky (1857–1935) was a Russian rocket pioneer. His study into the possibility of space travel led the way for the development of Russian space technology.

The First Satellite

The first human-made object ever to go into orbit around Earth was a Russian satellite called *Sputnik 1*. Launched in October 1957, *Sputnik 1* orbited Earth every 96 minutes at a height of more than 900 kilometers. People all around the world watched *Sputnik 1* pass overhead. The satellite could be seen in the night sky as a twinkling, moving object.

This Russian post card celebrates the launch of the first two Russian satellites.

satellite an object in orbit around Earth or another planet

A model of *Sputnik I* was displayed at the Russian Trade Fair in London.

Statistics for *Sputnik I*

- Launch date: October 4, 1957
- Burned up on re-entry to Earth's atmosphere: January 4, 1958
- Weight: 84 kilograms
- Diameter: 48 centimeters
- Orbit time: 96 minutes
- Maximum height above Earth: 940 kilometers
- Maximum speed: 29,000 kilometers per hour

Figure It Out

How would you solve these problems? You may use a calculator to help.

1. How many days after *Sputnik I* was launched did the satellite burn up on re-entry to Earth's atmosphere?

2. A family saw *Sputnik I* pass overhead at 7 P.M. At what times would the family be able to see the satellite overhead on the next three orbits?

3. How many times did *Sputnik I* orbit Earth in one day?

4. Estimate and then calculate how many orbits of Earth *Sputnik I* made in 23 days.

Animal Astronauts

Less than a month after the launch of *Sputnik 1*, Russia launched its second satellite, *Sputnik 2*. Inside *Sputnik 2* was a dog named Laika—the first living mammal to go into space. Over the years, other animals such as monkeys, cats, rats, fish, crickets, worms, and spiders have been sent into space. Sadly, not all of these animals survived.

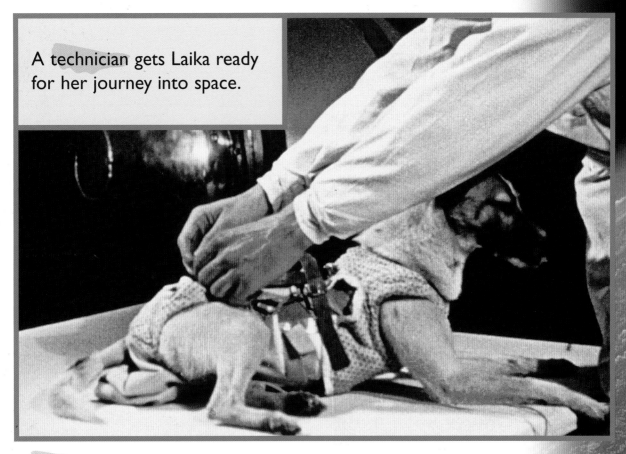

A technician gets Laika ready for her journey into space.

technician a person with knowledge and practical skills in a subject area

In 1960, two Russian dogs, Strelka (left) and Belka (right), became the first animals to travel to outer space and return to Earth.

Ham was the first chimpanzee in space. He blasted off from Cape Canaveral in January 1961. After he splashed down safely in the Atlantic Ocean, Ham was rewarded with an apple and half of an orange!

Lunar Landing

In 1959, two Russian rockets were launched toward the Moon. Each rocket released a cloud of bright orange gas, allowing astronomers to track the spacecraft. In January, *Luna 1* passed within 6,000 kilometers of the Moon and went into orbit around the Sun. In September, *Luna 2* reached its target, crash-landing onto the Moon's surface.

Sea of Serenity

Luna 2 took $33\frac{1}{2}$ hours to travel the 384,401 kilometers to the Moon. The spacecraft crashed near the Sea of Serenity.

astronomer a person who studies stars, planets, comets, and other objects found in space

Approximately how far do you think *Luna 2* traveled each hour? Choose the best of these answers:

A. 1,100 km
B. 11,000 km
C. 110,000 km

As space exploration captured the public's imagination, toys and other products with a space theme became very popular.

The Space Race

Both Russia and the United States wanted to be the first to send a person into space. In 1961, Russia narrowly won this "space race." On April 12, Major Yuri Gagarin spent 108 minutes orbiting Earth at a height of 301 kilometers. Less than a month later, Commander Alan Shepard, an American astronaut, traveled 184 kilometers into space and returned to Earth after 15 minutes.

Cosmonaut Yuri Gagarin's spaceship, *Vostok 1*, weighed 5 metric tons. It traveled at speeds of more than 28,000 kilometers per hour.

Did You Know?

Since 1962, April 12 has been a holiday in Russia.

cosmonaut   the Russian name for an astronaut

Alan Shepard became the first American in space on May 5, 1961. Ten years later, Shepard traveled to the Moon on *Apollo 14*.

In 1961, how much higher than Alan Shepard did Yuri Gagarin travel? For how much longer was Gagarin in space?

Space "Firsts"

By June 1963, Russia and America had each conducted six crewed space flights. However, the Soviets continued to create most of the "firsts" in space. They sent the first woman into orbit. They were the first to send two people into space at the same time. The first person to sleep in space was Russian. Overall, cosmonauts spent much more time in space than American astronauts.

The first woman in space was Valentina Tereshkova. She spent 70 hours orbiting Earth in June 1963. Before becoming a cosmonaut, Valentina worked in a textile mill. Her hobby was parachuting.

The First Space Flights

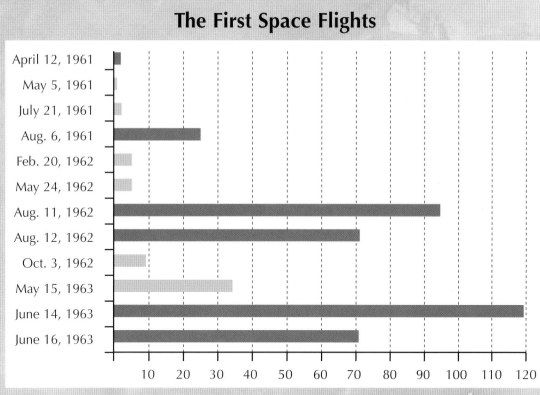

Launch Date

Date	Hours
April 12, 1961	
May 5, 1961	
July 21, 1961	
Aug. 6, 1961	
Feb. 20, 1962	
May 24, 1962	
Aug. 11, 1962	
Aug. 12, 1962	
Oct. 3, 1962	
May 15, 1963	
June 14, 1963	
June 16, 1963	

Hours

10 20 30 40 50 60 70 80 90 100 110 120

KEY

■ **By Russia**   ▨ **By America**

Look at the bar graph. Which flight was the longest? About how many days longer was it than the next longest flight? What else can you tell from the graph?

Walking in Space

The first space walk was made on March 18, 1965, by Alexei Leonov. While attached to one end of a 5-meter-long cable, the cosmonaut spent 12 minutes outside his spacecraft. During this time, the air pressure inside Leonov's space suit caused it to balloon out. At the end of the walk, Leonov had difficulty squeezing back into the spacecraft!

During his space walk, Leonov breathed oxygen that was carried through the cable from his spacecraft.

On February 3, 1984, American Bruce McCandless made the first space walk without a connecting cable. He wore a backpack with small thrusters, known as an MMU (Manned Maneuvering Unit).

How long after the first space walk was the first walk without a connecting cable? (Use years, months, and days in your answer.)

The main reason for space walking is to carry out repairs or maintenance outside a spacecraft or space station.

Race to the Moon

In 1966, a Russian spacecraft named *Luna 9*
became the first to make a soft landing on the Moon.
For several hours, *Luna 9* sent photographs of the
Moon's surface back to Earth. Over the next decade,
Russia carried out other *Luna* missions, but none
of them included cosmonauts. Every person who
has walked on the Moon has been American.

Luna 9 had four hinged
"petals" that opened to
reveal a television camera.

Did You Know?

Fom 1969 to 1972, six *Apollo* missions landed astronauts on the Moon.

On July 20, 1969, *Apollo 11* astronaut Neil Armstrong became the first person ever to set foot on the Moon. Watched by millions of people back on Earth, he said he was taking "one small step for (a) man; one giant leap for mankind."

Stationed in Space

Russia launched the world's first space station, *Salyut 1*, on April 19, 1971. A spaceship carrying the first crew arrived at the space station six weeks later. However, a fault in the docking equipment meant that the *Salyut* crew was not able to enter the space station. The second crew arrived on June 6 and stayed for 24 days. After only six months, *Salyut 1* re-entered Earth's atmosphere. Later, as technology improved, space stations were able to stay in space for much longer periods.

The longest single space mission was made by cosmonaut Valeri Polyakov. He lived on *Mir* from January 8, 1994, to March 22, 1995. In this photo, Polyakov (second from left) has just returned to Earth after breaking the space endurance record.

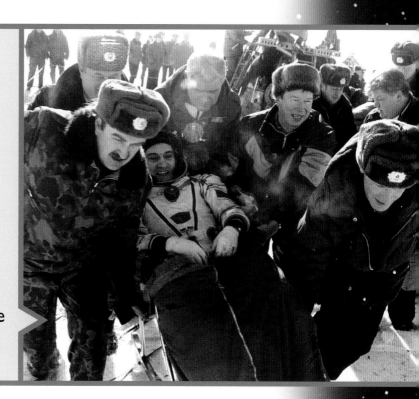

space station   a place where people can live and work in space for long periods

For how many months did *Mir* orbit Earth? For how many days did Valeri Polyakov live on *Mir*?

The Russian space station *Mir* orbited Earth from February 1986 to March 2001. Astronauts from 12 countries visited this space station.

Into the Future

In the early days of space exploration, Russia and America were rivals. Today, however, Russia and America are working together, along with many other countries, on the International Space Station.

A Russian cosmonaut (left) and an American astronaut (right) train together before leaving for the International Space Station.

Some Space "Firsts"

• Satellite in space	Oct. 4, 1957
• Animal in space	Nov. 3, 1957
• Crash-landing on Moon	Sept. 12, 1959
• Person in space	Apr. 12, 1961
• Person to sleep in space	Aug. 6, 1961
• Woman in space	Jun. 16, 1963
• Space walk	Mar. 18, 1965
• Soft-landing on Moon	Feb. 3, 1966
• Crash landing on Venus	Mar. 1, 1966
• Person on Moon	Jul. 20, 1969
• Space station	Apr. 19, 1971

Make a Space Timeline

To make a Space Timeline, you will need a ruler and a strip of paper at least 2 feet long.

1. Draw a line along the strip, as shown below.

2. To represent the months for 1957, draw 12 marks one-eighth of an inch apart.

3. Mark the "firsts" for 1957 on the timeline.

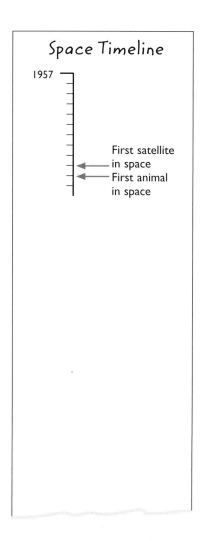

4. Draw a mark for each month in 1958 and 1959.

5. Mark the "first" from 1959 on the timeline.

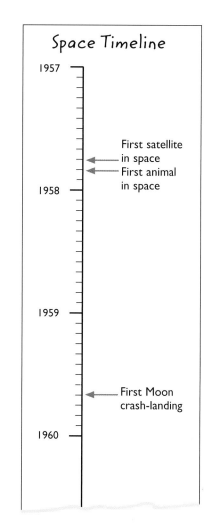

6. Keep going until your timeline shows all of the "firsts" on page 22.

Sample Answers

Page 7

1. 92 days
2. 8:36 P.M.; 10:12 P.M.; 11:48 P.M.
3. 15 times
4. 345 orbits

Page 11

B (33.5 hours x 11,000 km per hour = 368,500 km)

Page 13

117 km; 93 minutes

Page 17

18 years, 10 months, 16 days

Page 21

181 months (15 years, 1 month); 438 days (1 year, 2 months, 14 days)

> Find out about some of the important events in space during the 1970s and 1980s. Make a new timeline to show those events.

Index